BLOOD

BLOOD

SHANE MCCRAE

NOEMI PRESS
LAS CRUCES, NM

Noemi Press

P.O. Box 1330

Mesilla Park, NM 88047

www.noemipress.org

BLOOD

ISBN 978-1-934819-30-2

Cover photo by Matthea Harvey

Book design by Evan Lavender-Smith

Published by Noemi Press, Inc., a nonprofit literary organization

www.noemipress.org

For my father, for his parents, for their parents

CONTENTS

I should like to recommend that the stories be told in the language of the ex-slave, without excessive editorializing and "artistic" introductions on the part of the interviewer.... Care should be taken lest expressions such as the following creep in: "inflicting wounds from which he never fully recovered" (supposed to be spoken by an ex-slave).

authenticity

Finally, I should like to recommend that the words darky and nigger and such expressions as "a comical little old black woman" be omitted from the editorial writing. Where the ex-slave himself uses these, they should be retained.

—notes from an editor at the Federal Writers' Project

Whichever word you speak—
you owe to
destruction.

—Paul Celan (translated by John Felstiner)

HEADS

1. Escaped into the Swamp Then Made His Way Back to His Plantation

500 men in uniforms in army

uniforms 500 slaves   / 500

niggers we happy we nigger   *dialect*

soldiers marched on New Orleans   / And I was there I saw   *place*

after we niggers heads on sticks   *violence*

500 men in stolen uniforms or only   *belonging*

some of us but everything

Even ourselves we touched our touch

made stolen even   ] ★ *belonging / ownership*

our own bodies

In rags of uniforms from living even just ◯ a minute in them

The white folks in the city must have thought

It was something about our skin itself

Made clothes fall off

something about a nigger's skin

puts holes in everything he wears / 500   *Violence*

men in blood the blood

inside our bodies and the blood the dried

Spray of the blood of the white men we   violence

killed in the night   / And the black skin between

Like almost the

blood of the white men wearing from

the outside the

skin of us niggers

Against the blood inside us

And joy and something less than joy   contrast

kept us from washing our skin clean

We niggers we   wanted to be exactly

what the white men thought we were ←   identity

Kill them with that

and not with who we really were   / And now

I see it now and now I didn't see it then

Killing them we

made ourselves more

nigger their niggers and they

Killing us after

They made themselves   more innocent   innocence

More as

if they were gods I know about their gods

born from our heads on sticks   Violence

2. Captured and Returned to His Master

Some niggers isn't and they is

Never gonna be and them I known

And I remember best   violence

is niggers I seen dead   / Remember even

the breaths they was

always breathing breathing like how when

The master come   into the fields   the fields is changed   power

Their breathing come

Into the wind   as we was marching

and the wind was changed   opportunity

And it become like fruit we marching could

pluck from the air

The wind was fruit the air was trees

We marching could   eat and be satisfied

Them niggers isn't and they never was as we was

marching full of how we was

Each of us gonna kill a hundred white men each   violence

a hundred and we knew it was

14

More niggers anyway than whites

on the German Coast

[The death in us was bigger than the life in us] ✳

except for some of us   it seems like now

And them the niggers got their heads cut off

mounted on poles rep.

on the roads   into the city New Orleans

The white men recognized them mounted them

to make the air

Rotten and come from them / Rotten

animal
the meat in their necks hanging down ⌉

Like ivy on the gates of heaven   ⌉ Contrast

MERCY

My first thought was   *My baby's sick* / Wasn't a thought

really but that's what all that blood / Felt like

but all that blood

Really but all that blood   felt like my Mary getting / Sick on my hand

Wasn't a thought my first thought   was I wasn't / Was   I hadn't but I couldn't stop

After the first

Cut I couldn't stop

because it hurt

I couldn't stop / Hurting her because it hurt   I had to cut her head / All the way off

The marshals came with the Master

I wasn't

Thinking about mercy or love

Before that night   I never had the chance to love   / Anyone

she was the first   person I loved

[handwritten annotations: "hm" above "really but"; "irony" above "because it hurt"; "Violence" above "I had to cut her head / All the way off" (underlined); "Violence in the name of love" at bottom right; "mercy" circled; "I wasn't" double-underlined]

HOW TO RECOGNIZE IT

Master I learned from   more than anybody him

what love is how / To recognize it love

That's how I knew I was right to cut Mary's throat

Thinking of what he   did to me my

body what I knew he would

Do to Mary   to Priscilla cut   / Didn't just cut

and leave her body move

On to her sister   made   sure she was dead

I loved her   wanted her / Head to come off in my hands   wow

WITH THEIR BODIES

Father was white I knew he wasn't my / Father

was white and only love us

niggers with their bodies _Sex?_

didn't know / What love to give his child

Was white and left for

Oregon was white and sold   me to his brother sold

The farm and I went with it and   ⎤

                                     ⎦ _degrade_

the rye and hogs

And lost   two of his daughters to fever

on the boat to Oregon

And lost his wife in Oregon her head   ⎤

                                         ⎦ _Violence_

crushed by a wagon wheel

And the big house burned down

After they left they   all of them

had lived in

but   / The Master built another house

And called me in / Said   he wanted me

Close to the family   dead?

THE FIRST

Samuel was the first the first

Not Robert's child   Thomas was my first child / Samuel

children

was the first the Master fathered   *irony*

The first and every after

Samuel was the first

And in my belly

even in my belly / Looked like his father

riding / Low in my belly

like he was ashamed to be there   *power*

I was seventeen

The Master was a small man and an angry man

His wife had fallen down the stairs and died / His   *violence*

first wife Margaret Ann

And so he married an Elizabeth and started raping me   *casual*

Samuel was the first <u>the first of his not his</u>   *ownership*
                                                        identity

Children for every child he gave   Elizabeth for every

child who bore his name

I bore that white child's shadow

Samuel was the first

nigger I bore   *contrast*

WHITE

And see the same things told I don't   *differences*

see them the same way don't

See what the Master sees   / The same things

not the same things when a white man sees them

And Robert left the horses left

the Master's horses where

He knew they would be found and taken in   *escape*

And we   on foot our children and   ran to the river ran   across the river

in the snow

Stable across the road   from the Washington Hotel

In Covington Kentucky

in   / The snow I saw the snow

White falling from the sky

THE KNIFE

And Robert's mother she (escaped) / With us was with us in the house

And as the slave

catchers were breaking down the door were

climbing / Through the windows I

Begged her to help me kill the children   *violence*

Mary was already dead

Not Robert's but   named after

Mary Robert's mother

contrast

Not Robert's but the Master's / Who named a daughter Margaret Ann

rape

And raped me Margaret ←   *violence*

Garner whenever his wife got too

Pregnant

I begged her grabbed her hand my hands / Still wet with Mary's blood

And she said   *No*   and ran / Into another room

I looked   down at my hands

Decided then to use the shovel   violence?

CHILDREN

Was married but the Master kept me pregnant   *lack of control*

Robert my husband knew   he knew

The girls weren't his / Samuel wasn't his

But Thomas was the oldest was   *identity*

Robert and I were still   *age*   children ourselves / Robert

was fifteen I was sixteen when

Thomas was born

Except no nigger ever was a child   →   *responsibility*

Was when before my

father my / First master   sold the farm

And Robert even

then he always did a grown man's work

Except no nigger ever was grown   *irony*

And Robert he / Wanted me more

With every child that wasn't his   / And he   *ownership*

with every child that wasn't his

28

loved Thomas less

And when I went   after the boys / After Priscilla

with the shovel

To save them from the Master *irony*

I hit Thomas the hardest   WOW   violence

RUNNING

My legs were strong it doesn't matter

And prayed of anybody   hardest doesn't matter

And didn't stop   to pray when we were running let

The children piss their pants

My legs it doesn't matter

but running we left / Deeper and longer

prints in the snow / Running

hope

we made ourselves   easy to catch

And prayed

hardest it doesn't matter

violence

and / Watching the Master   carry Mary's body out

Slowly as if   Priscilla and the boys weren't bleeding

And wouldn't let not even   Robert anybody touch her

I felt the baby kick I felt her

pregnant?

running to be   buried in his arms

WITH THE INFANT MARY GARNER'S BODY IN HIS ARMS

Cont.

And carried her her   body back / On horseback back he

tried to carry her

Mary's body back / Across the river

Through Covington to Maplewood

Wanted to carry her argued   with the other slave

Catchers he tried

caring?

the Master tried   to argue

wanted

To argue carry her   and wouldn't give *control*

her body to the coroner   / Not

right away   but sat   down on the porch

Sobbing and

Choking on words the others / His

neighbors and the marshals

couldn't understand

As Mary's blood

Dried on his forearms

Tangled the hairs together _mixed up_

MARGARET GARNER IN CANAAN LAND

My father once   took me across the river   *history*

To Cincinnati I was seven not

My father but my master   on the ferry   *contrast*

and the lawyer said my lawyer after

Running   my lawyer in Ohio

Said I could have claimed my freedom then   *lost opp.*

White men in Cincinnati

would have fought to make me free

Lawyers like him

And I was seven had a woman's hands my hands

Were small and used to work   my father's wife would never do   / Were   *Master*

like my mother's hands

I touched my father's hand

in the moment he   lifted me to the roof of the bus   *care*

To sit me next to the driver

And my hand didn't burn or ache   / And no

part of me ached

And as we drove   the faces

of the white men in the street

All blurred together   just below my feet / I thought they would

trample me if I fell   Violence

TO PUNISH

To punish me   the Master

Shackled my legs together

On the boat to New Orleans

To punish me he never

Raped me again   *Irony*

Said   he the Master said he wouldn't

give me any more

Babies to kill   *Violence*

Was free and running still

When I cut Mary's throat

And killing her was running   / Was

shackled when I threw   Priscilla from the boat

And killing her was also

being chained

PRISCILLA

Named her Priscilla after / My mother

called her Cilla after what

The Master called my mother   *Violence*

And threw her into the Ohio

from a steamboat called   / The *Henry Lewis* ten months old

And she was nine months

when we ran   / And nine months crying on the floor

When the Master found us when

I cut her sister Mary's throat

And hit her   Cilla with a coal   *Violence*

shovel the flat of the blade / Swung

down   like I was putting out a fire

auditory, imagery

So hard I couldn't hear   the sound of her body   between the noise of the shovel

and the noise of the floor beneath her

And then the Master caught my arm pulled   me away

And then I heard her cry again

And jumped in after

I heard her had heard her crying   / After she hit the water

But didn't   in the water

hear her anymore

And I was happy then

And I was happy to be saved

2

THE BALLAD OF CATHAY WILLIAMS/WILLIAM CATHAY

A white man wouldn't less

He stripped me naked was

Whipping me know

I was a woman   got

A name just turn

It inside out

And I'm a man

How else I'm gonna know myself

When I am called

A white man wouldn't twice I had

Smallpox twice after   I enlisted   Serve

twice and had / To be

hospitalized both times

Ain't never once

no doctor nor no nurse

Discovered me

Man?

No for no white woman

I wouldn't have

nothing for her to see

She would want me to know she seen

And I was watching close

How else I'm gone to know myself

When I am called

And what she see is anyway

how is she gonna know for sure

Black man ain't got   *pretending*

a hole down there   *to be man*

How is she know he ain't

A white man born wrong inside out

and twice as big and mean   *difference*

And got a hole go twice as deep to hell

How is that woman sure

of anything at all

How else I'm etc

3

INDEPENDENCE (JAMES CAPE)

Master said *You*

In the army now

Jim how you like to join the army said

I got to tend

Horses   contrast

but the Rebels give us rifles send   control

Us niggers running

we / Niggers a running we / You

ever heard

Of the battle / Of Independence   irony

they

Send us running

up front to fight the Yankees / And the Yankees

kill us like they wasn't

Killing to set us free

Way up the other   side of Tennessee

One day we stopped a train took   Yankee / Money

I held my rifle on a Yankee

soldier he   just looked at me so scared

Like he never knew / What a rifle was

Power ✗

until he saw one in my hands

SHAME (MARY ARMSTRONG)

Old Polly Cleveland was   she was a Polly devil if

Ever there was one killed / My little sister just for crying tore   *Violence*

her diaper off

Whipped her to death was

nine months old when I was ten I got her back

Busted her eyeball with a rock

Belonged then to her daughter then

her daughter set me free   / In '63   *Freedom*

And I went down to Texas found my mamma

It was still   slave time in Texas but I had my papers

when   / A white man put me on the block / I held my papers up

I wouldn't let him take them made him   stand to look   / I reck-

on any

white man there if we had been alone

He would've snatched those papers quick / I reckon it was

shame that saved me   white?
                            Shame?

so I don't never feel no shame

MONEY (LUCRETIA ALEXANDER)

I saw them once the

Yankees saw them from

A long way off

And they were riding coal

black horses and / I hollered out I said

I see / Something

and told my mistress what I saw / I saw

them didn't know

What I was seeing

and before I knew it my

Mistress had thrown a sack of silver on me so

Heavy it knocked me down / Told

me to hide it sent me running

During the war

Jeff Davis gave   Confederate

Money out

but / It died on the folks' hands   confederate
                                                            money

The silver rattled as I ran it sounded like

a chained dog jumping   Freedom

TALK (MARY ANDERSON)

From when I was a slave is

why / I talk like white   race

folks my association and my training

Master and / Missus they gave us good

Treatment and all their family there   irony
                                             contrast

And every Sunday gathered us for Sunday

morning breakfast said

Good morning children and / The slave   contrast

children dipped up their food with mussel shells ∫

⌈ It was a black cloud coming when the Yankees came ⌉ △

I heard a sound like thunder boom boom boom / Asked

Missus was it going to rain

She sent me to the icehouse for

Some pickles and preserves

The slaves

Were whooping and   hollering and

acting like they were crazy when

The Yankees told them they were free   the Yankees were

Shaking hands   calling them Dinah   Sarah   Sam   *identity*

SEEDS (ISAAC ADAMS)

After the war half

about half   of Master Sack's

Negroes they left

the other half

Stayed on and they were free

now so they paid him shares / Stayed

on and some   eventually some

bought the mules he loaned them some

The land he let them work

And some his tools

for tearing up that land

for harvesting the seeds

RECONSTRUCTING

After the war   the army the   Confederate our

boys in gray   / Our boys in rags   *identity*

after the war in uniforms

Had fighting in them still   / And no

Yankees to fight

And niggers mostly everywhere   / Government mostly everywhere enforcing nigger rights

And it was nigger rights got Grant elected president

You sometimes seen them fifty men a hundred / Our

boys chase down a pack of niggers

Like they was the cavalry or the Klan

Our boys you sometimes

It wasn't guns but mostly knives but mostly rifle butts   *Violence*
Still

You stab a man you   break his skull

you want that man to see you

That man won't know he's   / Nothing

if he can't look you in the eye

REVIVAL

Was a revival a was   / A tent revival the

preacher he had

Preacher he couldn't stop himself

From showing off his baby's corpse   why

He held it up he never   held it any other way

but up and facing

The congregation

and he preached on how it bore the signs of the Devil   child

But looked just like a Klansman

And how our Savior comes disguised

The baby's head was

Big as a grown man's   / The baby's

eyes its mouth

Were smaller than a baby's

and it had a growth   / A thick white crown

on top of its head

and two horns at the base of the crown   / The preacher held it up

devil

The hour it was born

he said   / Our Savior comes disguised   / Like a thief in the night

And in our time

our Savior He has stepped   *religion*

down from the cross

And He must set the cross on fire

TO SHOW

Klan didn't want   most of the time they wasn't want / To rape nobody most

of the time the Klan they want is scare   people but first they had to kill 'em

Kill him you got a nigger scared for life

Kill him you got   / Sometimes most anyway the Klan or any white men make a woman show

And always in the road

Making her show or when it was the Klan or any white men raping her   was always in the road

most always in the middle   to be seen   / Most always in the night

when nobody was looking

Except her man and was the Klan already whipped the babies   wasn't

Never a baby born too

Young to remember

But was whipping the babies didn't make no difference was the Klan

They wanted was the woman in the road   they wasn't

Wanted to rape her they or any white men knew

I seen it with my eyes a man will throw his crying baby to the ground

To watch his woman cry

WHY THEY BURNED HIM

Owed him his wages when he asked

the white man stood and shook

a hammer in his face

And so he hit the white man with the hammer   *Violence*

And ran he didn't

check to see if the white man was dead a black man

hits a white man and the white man dies

The white man dies the black man raped his wife   he ran

South to his momma dug himself a hole

under her porch

And wouldn't leave it he was barefoot in

Shit when the white men found him   / He stank so bad

They couldn't hang him didn't want those feet

over their heads

Violence

That's why they burned him

THE CROWD SHOUTED AND HOLLERED

Cut off before

burning him his

[handwritten: Violence]

Fingers his fingers off   wanted his fingers

Fresh and could sell them

Later in town

and didn't want his fingers burned   *[handwritten: why]*

black   / Cut off his fingers held   his fingers high

Mostly a clear day and

the crowd   shouted and hollered and

They couldn't see the fingers there was so much blood could

only see the blood   could see

The fingers there   was so much blood / They couldn't tell the fingers from   *[handwritten: difference?]*

the white man's fingers   / It

looked as if the white man had

cut his own fingers off

But who what   sane man

would cut his own fingers off   *[handwritten: Violence!]*

4

THE LAST LETTER I GOT (W. L. BOST)

My boy he was a beautiful and skin

~~differences~~

~~As white as any white boy's skin~~ says he has joined the navy

when

He was he was a boy he was   seven or eight I took

Him into town   and the conductor made me put him in the front

of the streetcar thought

My boy he was a white boy I was just   Identity

caring for him   my boy   / I told him *Tell him*

I'm your daddy but

he didn't say

Anything   the conductor   Power

Would have believed him he was white

Pretty as white and anything

White folks believe you anything / He

63

says he hasn't spoken to a

differences

colored girl in years

5

BROTHER

Proem: *Whose Story of Us We Is Told Is Us*

Brother is we is each of us we ghosts

Brother of white folks we

don't never known us brother we

Because we never doesn't fits

Nowhere we brother

doesn't fits in bodies

identity

Our bodies we is always walking leaking

like a ghost can't be a body in one place

But every eyes   / Catches and pulls at it

Like every eyes in any

white folks is another

Hole in our bodies

attention

Brother   / Is we is never known them close

Up close   whose ghosts we brother leaking is

Whose story of us we is told is us   is water in a fist

loss

67

absence

Brother we not the fist

we not the water

we the thirst

1. The First Part of the Earth

We the thirst   brother the

we water from the inside from the lips

From nowhere to the lips

We water inside brother we to say it water

from the inside   *power*

thirst and we   / Can't never have us   like it's

water got a color   got a black   *color*

Brother we hungry water like

We was the first   / Part of the Earth

It's we don't even know

How any we could satisfy our hunger   what

Satisfy us   because it ain't / Was nothing here before us brother the

Thing meant to satisfy it come before

the hungry thing   / So that the hungry thing will find it there

And known what it was for

2. The One Whose Mother Was Black and the One Whose Mother Was White

We known what it was for

and tell it brother let me tell it us   / Was it was for

And in the morning of the sun in the rising sun / Our faces to the sun

Or let me tell it you was born

Brother was winter I had asked for you / Brother was spring   the sun so much

it didn't none of me believe the blue

Come out of the black

Brother until I was if I'm

A grown man now I thought the sky was two   differences

skies let   / Me tell it us two skies   two brothers one / The black sky

one a color don't come any part of black

Tell it we known what light

Was for

                                                            race

I can't see   in my skin   our father's face

3. Gone Sleeping in Me Till I Die

I can't see   in my skin our father's face / Brother or any other face

Of any like me brother the same black

Brother you got his skin or his but dark-

er but it's darker so it's his

Darker from where

it's in the first place black keeps black   darker from where

It's white or lighter from

black my whole families disappear   / My mother's and our father's families they

The white ones and the black ones gone / Brother they sleeping

Gone sleeping in me till I die   / Brother and it my skin turns gray   and dust

No skin the family of my skin

But if my skin

separates me from you

brother it does not keep me

4. Keep Us

Brother it does not keep us brother it

Keep us like wind keep a tree a tree

Rooted and still get never any rest

Brother it I was raised to think Brazil

Our father he   abandoned me

went to Brazil

Brother I'm sorry   for the stories I was told   rumours lie

Brother the stories keep me even though I

Know they are stories even   kept away   / Our father him from him

Brother it keep us like a pond keep leaves

from trees on the pond they

Rotting in the thing they lived on

rot   [So slow it's almost like forever] ✈

Brother our father me and him / That's how it love

keep us together

5. Chicken Bones Piled Up High

Keep us together brother is ~~our bodies is a grave~~ / Got   piled up chicken bones in there

Brother is us our bodies is

the shards of them

Shards like they glass bad stuck

Violence

Bad shards of bone in the fried skin   / Ate up so much of the skin we brother like

We ain't got human bones no more / We got

chicken bones piled up high

Might as well wear a sign we got

why

Chicken bones piled up high   / Get never any rest

from chewing night and day on glass   / Chicken bones piled up high

brother is like we graves   / Is we was born in bodies was

Graves first

like how we get our bodies if we ain't

poverty eating

put chicken bones in it

6. Whole

Put chicken bones in it   and watermelon bones / We brother we

water men bones   / Is bones don't say

or lift   or drag our bodies under is

Our bones is masks

Give us deceiving shapes   our bones is flesh

Give us the (sameness) we   brother we got between us give

Us how we (separate) ourselves

Brother we water and our bones is rocks in us

We rivers and our bones is trash   / Is sometimes bones themselves

from bodies thrown in is   / Brother we borrow it

Is brother we to say we thought / To borrow it believed

to couldn't grow no human bones ourselves   *arc not human*

If we was given our whole lives

7. From Which Others

If we were given our whole lives   / Brother if we

were given if / We given lives   brother our even our

Lives is our even our

if we were given brother to / Live them a black

lives brother if / Black lives were not   but would we want them

different were the

Standard the facelessness against

Which lives are measured facelessness

A white face even our   / Brother if we were given

but we couldn't be   / Our lives the given from which others receive the gift

Nobody

brother gets it whole

But if we were would you   / Brother   I know it

I would

not grant that wholeness to anybody else

8. Blood Familiar

Anybody else   / Brother I would more recognize myself

In anybody else   brother except I see   *together*

My shoulders in your shoulders my

Body in your clothes   but where your skin shows brother your

Face and your hands

your skin   / Darker than mine   *different*

which drifts and changes in the sun

Your skin our father's skin

brother my little brother your

Name his name   the name he would have given me / If he had been allowed to choose

I recognize   / My name when I hear yours

but when I see / Your face   your hands

the hands I love   the face I love   the skin I love
     vs white master
Brother you are made strange by love

76

9. Asked

Brother you are made strange by love and was [*master?*]

Two when I asked for you our father for

You maybe I was three

was three I asked

Him for a brother brother by the time you came

Was three and gone had been   / Taken away gone

by the time you came   / To Texas by the time you came / Or his our father's memory

He tells me he remembers me

Watching you in your crib

brother I don't remember watching you

But grew up   when I thought of you

Imagining you there   / A baby I imagined looked like you

and that was who I grew up loving

And when I met you you were not my brother [*Family*]

10. His Face When I Was Looking

When I met you you were not my brother

Brother at sixteen you   at thirteen brother when

I finally tracked our father down   lost

After I tracked our father down   my mother

Family

She told me she had always seen his / Gestures in mine   / In the way

I turned my head to look away

And she had never told me that before   and said she always wanted to / Brother

I had no memories of you

No way to know or guess

No pictures of our father in the house / His

face when I was looking

your face when I   Family

Had found you

I was raised an only child   I didn't think

To look in the mirror or to look away

11. Brother I Was Taken Away and Told Our Father Had Abandoned Me

My face our father's when I look away   / Or my

body your body when I move   Family

Mine in the house alone   / In the house I grew up in / Brother   in the house not no one not

one brother one / Of any in the house one skin   of any matching skin   / Or tell

me brother what   the difference is between / The body and the face   / Looking

not any brother in the house   / Not any blood   / Or blood but not his blood   family

Brother not yours   the difference between

[Resemblance and resemblance] brother since

your hands move like his hands   or am I both

You and our father

rising do I rise

to walk away

12. We Become Impossible

Walking away   / Or never when I pictured him

Walking just disappeared   never just walking

out of the room   / Our father when I pictured him

leaving my mother me

Pictured him brother disappeared   / From the white room   from the hospital was there

To see me born and after gone just vanished I was told

That story brother I was told

he didn't come

The story changed

From year to year when I was growing / Up

brother till when people asked I said

I didn't have a father he   Family

became impossible

Brother I don't

visit because I can't

I do not have a father and I love him   ron

Coda: Love Between Men

I don't   brother I do not have a

brother we's   / Ghost makers any bringing babies

Into this world

brother it was my

Great-uncle wrestled   the gun from my mother's father's hands

The day her family got the news

Brother it was my   great-uncle it was a

Tenant he had evicted this was years   / Later

from the window of an empty

Apartment shot him through the neck   Violence

He wrestled the   gun from my mother's father's hands

Brother and you were born

And blood sprayed from the artery

                              Contrast
A rose

like if the Lord had stopped

making in the middle of making red

<u>roses</u>

✈ [and never made their boundaries]

6

AFTER THE UPRISING

Well some of us escaped

into the swamp and some of us

Snuck back quick to our masters   and our masters knew

who stayed and who

Ran with the rebels to   / Kill with the rebels   *Violence*

still   / Some of us snuck back quick

we knew we valuable $

Besides you kill a man you can't

Murder him forever

not even for that stretch of forever

white folks own

but only negroes get

old in   and some of us

snuck back heavy

like how the first thing I

Done with my freedom was I thought

Who do I got to kill   *knowledge*

to get all the way free   *Freedom*

And it was   more people than it was

alive in the world

NOTES

"Heads" and "After the Uprising" are based on the German Coast Uprising of 1811. I am indebted to Daniel Rasmussen for his book on the subject, *American Uprising: The Untold Story of America's Largest Slave Revolt.*

Steven Weisenburger's *Modern Medea: A Family Story of Slavery and Child Murder from the Old South* was an invaluable resource to me as I was writing the poems in section one.

"The Ballad of Cathay Williams William Cathay": Cathay Williams was the first African-American woman to enlist as a soldier in the United States Army. She did so in 1866, disguised as a man, and served for almost two years.

"Seeds (Isaac Adams)," "Money (Lucretia Alexander)," Talk (Mary Anderson)," "Shame (Mary Armstrong)," "The Last Letter I Got (W. L. Bost)" and "Independence (James Cape)" were all adapted from slave narratives collected by the Federal Writers' Project in the 1930s.

I took some of the facts and details in "Reconstructing," "Revival," "To Show," "Why They Burned Him" and "The Crowd Shouted and Hollered" from Philip Dray's history of lynching in America, *At the Hands of Persons Unknown.*

ACKNOWLEDGMENTS

Thanks to Oliver de la Paz, Derek Gromadzki, J. Michael Martinez, Melissa McCrae, and Carmen Giménez Smith for their advice and counsel. Thanks to Matthea Harvey for taking the photograph that appears on the cover. Thanks to the editors and staffs of the following journals, in which some of these poems first appeared, sometimes in different versions. And special thanks to everyone at the Academy of American Poets' Poem-A-Day project and *Gulf Coast* for allowing "Whose Story of Us We Is Told Is Us" and "The First Part of the Earth," respectively, to be reprinted by *At Length*.

At Length: "Brother"
Barn Owl Review: "Talk (Mary Anderson)"
Bat City Review: "The Crowd Shouted and Hollered"
Bellingham Review: "The Last Letter I Got (W. L. Bost)"
Denver Quarterly: "Mercy," "Running"
Fence: "Money (Lucretia Alexander)" and "Shame (Mary Armstrong)"
Gulf Coast: "The First Part of the Earth"
Indiana Review: "With Their Bodies"
Kenyon Review Online: "After the Uprising"
Petri Press: "Heads"
RealPoetik: "How to Recognize It"
Saltgrass: "To Show"
The Spoon River Poetry Review: "Reconstructing" and "Revival"
Thumbnail Magazine: "Independence (James Cape)"
Typo: "Children," "Margaret Garner in Canaan Land" and "With the Infant Mary Garner's Body in His Arms"
Zone 3: "The First" and "Seeds (Isaac Adams)"

"Whose Story of Us We Is Told Is Us" and "The Ballad of Cathay Williams William Cathay" were originally published as part of the Academy of American Poets' Poem-A-Day project.

Some of these poems appear in a chapbook, *In Canaan*, published by Rescue Press.

And my gratitude forever to the Mrs. Giles Whiting Foundation for its support.